101 Aı
Do in ıreıand

MW01295036

© 2018 101 Amazing Things

Introduction

So you're going to Ireland, huh? You are so very lucky indeed! You are sure in for a treat because Ireland is truly one of the most magical countries on the face of the earth.

This guide will take you on a journey from the major cities like Dublin and Belfast through to picturesque areas of the Irish countryside, and just about everywhere else in between.

In this guide, we'll be giving you the low down on:
- the very best things to shove in your pie hole, from incredible street markets through to Irish favourites like Guinness stew
- incredible festivals, whether you would like to be entertained at the Dublin Fringe Festival, or you'd prefer to party in the wilderness at Electric Picnic
- the coolest historical and cultural sights that you simply cannot afford to miss from a church that dates way back to the 7th century to historic castles

- the most incredible outdoor adventures, whether you'd like to climb to the highest peak in Ireland or you'd enjoy a night kayaking experience on an Irish lake
- the places where you can party like a local and make new friends
- and tonnes more coolness besides!

Let's not waste any more time – here are the 101 most amazing, spectacular, and coolest things not to miss in Ireland!

1. Learn about the History of Guinness

Without a doubt, one of the most iconic things about the Irish is their love of Guinness, and one of the most iconic attractions in the capital is the Guinness Storehouse in Dublin. Across seven floors, you can learn about the history of the Guinness brand, how Guinness has advertised itself over the years, the process of making Guinness, and there is even a Guinness bar at the very top where you can taste the magic for yourself.

(St James's Gate, Ushers, Dublin 8; www.guinness-storehouse.com/en)

2. Peruse the Aisles of English Market in Cork

When you're in Cork and you want to fill your stomach, for us there is one place that stands head and shoulders above the rest and it's not a Michelin star restaurant but a humble place called English market. These days, you can purchase all kinds of foods here, but we still think that it's the traditional foods that stand out. Don't miss out on sampling some drisheen, the Irish version of blood pudding, which typically has more of a gelatinous consistency than other blood puddings.

(Princes St, Centre, Cork; www.englishmarket.ie)

3. Visit a 1000 Year Old Stone Church

Gallarus Oratory is a church like no other that you have seen before. This is no grand building with ornate frescoes. In fact, it's a very simple stone structure, but what makes it special is that it dates way back to the 7th or 8th century, and that makes it the oldest preserved church to be found anywhere in Ireland. A legend has it that if you climb out of the oratory window, your soul will be cleansed.

(Dingle Penninsula, Dingle, Co. Kerry; www.gallarusoratory.ie)

4. Head Back to 1904 Dublin at the Bloomsday Festival

Dublin is a literary city and perhaps the most famous book to emerge from Dublin is Ulysses by James Joyce. The annual Bloomsday Festival is a celebration of the writer through the recreation of events in 1904, when the book is set. On June 16th each year, you'll find James Joyce themed pub crawls, dramatisations of the text, and some hardcore fans even host 36 hour readings of the whole Ulysses book.

(www.bloomsdayfestival.ie)

5. Enjoy Some Beers at the Rising Sons Microbrewery

While in Ireland, it won't be too long before you realise that the local population certainly does like a drink. Of course, Guinness is ever popular, but if you feel like trying something away from the mainstream, we highly recommend a small microbrewery in Cork that goes by the name of Rising Sons. Everything is produced fresh on site, and that means the taste is always fresh and clean. And if you fancy a bite with your pint, they also make a killer pizza.

(Cornmarket St, Centre, Cork; www.risingsonsbrewery.com)

6. Keep Yourself Toasty and Warm With Donegal Tweeds

Walk around the beautiful county of Donegal, and you might just notice that the men there are dressed extraordinarily well. This is in no small part down to the prevalence of Donegal tweed, which has been produced into caps, vests, and suits for centuries in this part of Ireland. If you are a guy who really prides himself on looking his best (or you know one), an indulgence for your trip to Ireland simply has to be a custom made Donegal tweed suit.

7. Try Night Kayaking at Lough Hyne

So, everybody has heard of kayaking, and maybe you've even tried sea kayaking for yourself. This is certainly a wonderful way to explore the waters of Ireland, but night kayaking at Lough Hyne is something altogether different because people come from far and wide to try the night kayaking here. The magical thing about this experience is that the lake actually lights up with bioluminescence so it's like paddling through the stars.

8. Visit Ireland's Oldest City, Waterford

History buffs need to put the small city of Waterford, the oldest city in Ireland, on their must visit list. This charming place has records dating way back to Viking times, and you can actually tour the Viking Triangle and its historic sights. The city is most famous for its incredible crystal and the company, Waterford Crystal, who have created chandeliers for Westminster Abbey and Windsor Castle. Don't leave before popping into the Waterford Crystal Visitor Centre.

9. Take in a Live Rugby Match

If you are at all sporty, there's only one sport that you need to make sure that you're acquainted with on a trip to Ireland, and that is rugby. Rugby is the official national sport, and it's a great idea to see what the big deal is at a live match. A huge stadium in Dublin is called the Aviva Stadium, and this is where most of the important international matches are held. With a capacity to hold 57,000 raucous rugby fans, you can guarantee that the atmosphere for any match is totally electric.

(Lansdowne Rd, Dublin 4; www.avivastadium.ie)

10. Drink Like Royalty at the House Hotel

In our opinion, Galway is a very underrated city with a bit of everything to keep everyone happy. As soon as we arrive in Galway, the first thing that we do is head to the bar of the House Hotel. This is probably the best cocktail bar in the whole city, but there is one cocktail that we like above all the rest, and that's The Duchess. The drink was created to mark the visit of the Duchess of Cambridge to Galway, and it contains a delicious mix of gin and elderflower that is topped up with champagne.

(Spanish Parade, Latin Quater, Galway City; www.thehousehotel.ie)

11. Get Back to Nature in Connemara National Park

Connemara National Park is one of only six national parks in all of Ireland, and we think it's the ultimate place for nature lovers in the country. In this park, you'll find almost 3000 hectares of mountains, heaths, bogs, grasslands, and woodlands. Head to the visitor centre, and you'll discover a number of trails for all abilities. If you manage to climb to the top of 400 metre high Diamond

Hill, you'll discover views of distant islands as well as Kylemore Abbey.

(Mweelin, Letterfrack, Co. Galway; www.connemaranationalpark.ie)

12. Have a Glamping Experience at the Wild Atlantic Camp

There are certainly enough camping sites dotted around Ireland for you to have a great camping experience, but if you are still on the fence about camping and you'd like to dip your toe in with some glamping, you have this option at the Wild Atlantic Camp in Donegal. No tents are involved at all, and you get to stay in a heated wooden pod, which is just luxurious enough to feel like you are roughing it, but it's still out there in the wilderness.

(Main St, Creeslough, Co. Donegal; www.wildatlanticcamp.ie)

13. Listen to Some Smooth Sounds at Cork Jazz Festival

When you've heard just about as much of the Irish fiddle as you can handle, you might be interested in listening to some of the smoother sounds of jazz music, and the annual Cork Jazz Festival offers the perfect opportunity for this. This is Ireland's premier jazz festival, and it takes place annually at the end of October. Hundreds of musicians are attracted to the festival each year, and there are concerts in city venues as well as on the streets. Will you be part of it?

(www.guinnessjazzfestival.com)

14. Cheer on Locals at The Liffey Swim

The Liffey is the main river that intersects Dublin, and each year in August there are hundreds of brave souls who take part in the Liffey Swim, a race across the river in the open waters. There are races for men and women, as singles and in teams. As the temperature of the river water is rarely very warm, the competitors need as much encouragement as they can possibly get. The atmosphere on the riverside on race day is incredible, so why not join in with the fun, and cheer on the brave souls in the water?

15. Eat Fresh Seafood at Oscar's in Galway

Ireland is surrounded by water, and so it should come as no surprise that Ireland offers some of the very best seafood in the world. If you are on the hunt for a delicious seafood dinner to remember, trust us when we tell you that Oscar's in Galway is the place to be. This charming seafood bistro has won numerous awards with a menu that changes with the seasonality of ingredients. The Clare Island salmon tartar is a particular highlight, and the catch of the day never disappoints.

(Dominick Street Lower, Galway; www.oscarsseafoodbistro.com)

16. Browse Through the Milk Market of Limerick

Limerick is a small city, and yet it's a place where you can find anything and everything. When you are in need of some grub on a Saturday, there are plenty of options to be found, but our first choice is always the Milk Market, which has its origins in the 19th century. This is one of the premier farmers' markets in the country, and you'll find everything from local produce, like Irish butters and cheeses, to more exotic fare. So whether you fancy a cheese sandwich or a spicy curry in the beautiful setting of the market, you'll be able to find something that appeals to you at the Milk Market.

(www.milkmarketlimerick.ie)

17. Visit Ireland's Oldest Operational Lighthouse

Ireland's oldest operational lighthouse, and actually one of the world's oldest lighthouses full stop, Hook, is well worth a visit, and can be found in picturesque Wexford. The existing lighthouse tower dates all the way back to the 12th century, and some kind of beacon has existed on the site since the 5th century. Take the guided tour, and you'll have the chance to get to grips with history in action.

(Churchtown, Hook Head, Co. Wexford; http://hookheritage.ie)

18. Tuck Into a Big Plate of Coddle

Coddle is exactly the kind of food that an Irish mother would cook for you. It's essentially a dish that combines all different kinds of leftovers in one plate, which means that it can vary from plateful to plateful, but typically it includes chopped sausages, bacon, potato and onions. Fortunately, you don't have to be part of a traditional Irish family to enjoy a plate of coddle, simply head to The Boxty House in Dublin.

(20 Temple Bar, Dublin; http://boxtyhouse.ie)

19. Discover Ireland's Past at Bunratty Castle

Bunratty Castle is one of the most complete and authentic medieval fortresses that can be found in Ireland. Built in 1425, this fortress still contains art, furnishings, and tapestries from that period, and it's a must visit for all history buffs on a trip to the Emerald Isle. The castle also regularly serves up medieval banquets in the evening time, and so it's a wonderful place to have a unique experience while listening to harp music and sipping on mead.

(Bunratty West, Bunratty, Co. Clare)

20. See the Largest Stalactite in the Northern Hemisphere

As you descend into Doolin Cave, you will leave the contemporary world as you know it behind you, and have the opportunity to explore a world from 350 million years ago. In fact, because this cave contains the largest hanging stalactite in the whole of the northern hemisphere, it's one of the most exciting cave experiences anywhere. The stalactite is an impressive 7.3 metres in length, and it weighs more than ten tonnes. Below the stalactite, there is a glimmering pond where you can see its reflection.

(Craggycorradan East, Doolin, Co. Clare; http://doolincave.ie)

21. Walk the Meadows of Burren Nature Sanctuary

For endless days in nature, Ireland is the perfect destination. Located just outside of the village of Kinvara, you can find the Burren Nature Sanctuary, the kind of outdoor paradise that has a bit of something for everybody. There are vast stretches of meadows with wildflowers and orchids, there is an ancient woodland with many trails through the forest, there is a farm where visitors can put donkeys, sheep, micropigs, and more, and there is even a café that uses seasonal, local ingredients to cook up tasty meals and snacks.

(Cloonnasee, Co. Galway; www.bns.ie)

22. Have a Dance at the Galway Early Music Festival

The Galway Early Music Festival has to be one of the most unique festivals in Ireland. You can forget big name artists and electronica, because this festival is a celebration of European music from the 12th to the 18th centuries. The festival is held annually over the mid-May weekend when you can experience concerts, workshops, and masterclasses that will take you on an artistic journey back in time through the medieval, Renaissance, and Baroque periods.

(http://galwayearlymusic.com)

23. Climb Aboard the SS Nomadic

The ship that was built to ferry passengers to the doomed Titanic ship is now the last remaining of the White Star vessels, and you can discover this part of history for yourself by actually climbing aboard the ship in Belfast. Unlike her sister ship, the SS Nomadic went on to perform many years of service, and only retired in the 1960s. You can now take tours and view exhibitions aboard the ship, and walk the same steps as those sadly fated Titanic passengers.

(Hamilton Dock, Queens Road, Belfast; www.nomadicbelfast.com)

24. Join in With the Fun of the Rose of Tralee

The Rose of Tralee is a festival that is celebrated in Irish communities all over the world, but it has its roots in the town of Tralee in County Kerry. The festival takes its inspiration from a 19th century ballad of the same name, which describes a woman as "lovely and fair". The idea of the festival is to find the local woman who most captures the essence of the ballad. These days, each county in Ireland selects its own rose, and those women then compete to be in the ultimate Rose of Tralee.

(www.roseoftralee.ie)

25. Cycle Along the Great Western Greenway

If your idea of the perfect afternoon is putting your foot to the pedal and discovering the countryside of Ireland on a pushbike, you're in luck because the country has many great trails designed with cyclists in mind, and the Great

Western Greenway is one of these. The 42 kilometre trail is the longest off road cycling trail in Ireland. As you cycle, you'll get to take in views of the Nephin Beg mountain range, Clare Island, and Clew Bay.

(www.greenway.ie)

26. Discover Ancient Treasures at the Hunt Museum

If you find yourself in Limerick on a rainy day and you aren't sure what to do, a trip to the Hunt Museum is bound to be rewarding. This museum is the home of the personal collection of the Hunt Family, and we particularly like it because there is so much diversity within the collection that there is bound to be something that grabs your attention. In the collection of around 2500 pieces, you will find paintings by Picasso, artefacts from Stone Age Ireland, and even dresses by Irish designers.

(Rutland St, Limerick; www.huntmuseum.com)

27. Catch a Film at the Dublin International Film Festival

Yes, the sightseeing and hopping from pub to pub in Dublin is totally awesome, but sometimes you just want to kick back and watch a great movie. If you love nothing more than to lean back into a comfortable cinema seat, make sure that your trip to Dublin coincides with the Dublin International Film Festival, which takes place every February. Each year, you'll be able to catch the most exciting world cinema as well as films from up and coming Irish filmmakers, plus workshops, panels, and Q&A events.

(www.diff.ie)

28. Get to Grips with Rural Ireland at the Museum of Country Life

Rural life has been something extremely important in the story of Ireland as a nation, and this is never more apparent than when you visit the Museum of Country Life in the village of Turlough. This museum covers country life from 1850-1950 with a staggeringly impressive range of temporary and permanent exhibitions. Inside the museum, you can learn about folk life and folklore, how rural life in Ireland was shaped by its natural resources, the activities in the home and on the farm, and the realities of working on the land.

(www.museum.ie/Country-Life)

29. Watch Dolphins at the Shannon Estuary

When you think of dolphin watching, you might think of places with warmer climes such as Mexico, but actually, there is a huge population of bottlenose dolphins off the coast of Ireland by the Shannon Estuary. It's actually here that many dolphins give birth to their young, and if you are lucky, you might even get to see these young dolphins on a trip out on to the ocean.

30. Dance, Dance, Dance at Electric Picnic

If you fancy getting on board with Ireland's summer festival scene, Electric Picnic is something that you really have to experience. This festival takes place at the end of August each year in Stradbally, and it's often thought of as Ireland's answer to Glastonbury. There's a huge amount of live music at the festival with a leaning towards more electronic acts. Artists that have performed in the past include The Chemical Brothers, New Order, Royksopp, and Bjork.

(www.electricpicnic.ie)

31. Find Paradise on Dog's Bay

When you think of perfect beach paradises around the world, Ireland might not be the first country that comes to mind, but we don't think that any beach lovers will have a smidge of disappointment on a trip to Ireland. There are numerous lovely beaches, but we are particularly enamoured by Dog's Bay in County Galway. Dog's Bay has crystal clear waters and is perfectly safe for swimming – you just might want to visit in the summer for warmer swimming temperatures.

32. Take in a Cultural Event at Triskel Arts Centre

Although Ireland is in many ways a very traditional place, this is not to say that there is no contemporary arts scene to be found in the country, and when we want an injection of contemporary culture, we always head to the Triskel

Arts Centre in Cork. Housed in a beautiful Christchurch building, there is always something going on. The arthouse cinema screens cool films every day, and you'll find contemporary dance, poetry readings, and more.

(Tobin St, Centre, Cork; http://triskelartscentre.ie)

33. Learn to Cook Like the Irish

Tucking into Irish food is all well and good, but how much more impressive would it be if you could actually learn to cook traditional Irish dishes so that you could host Irish dinner parties at home? Pretty darn impressive, we reckon. And that's why you need to know about Dublin Cookery School. This is the perfect school for tourists because they have evening or one day classes, so you don't have to commit to a whole semester. Plus, you can learn how to make scrumptious local plates such as soda bread and beef stew.

(2 Brookfield Terrace, Blackrock, Co. Dublin; www.dublincookeryschool.ie)

34. Discover the Unspoiled Beaches of Achill Island

Ireland is, of course, an island in itself, but there are also many smaller islands away from the mainland that are well worth exploring. Achill Island is the largest of all the islands off the coast, and it can be found just off the coast of mainland County Mayo. With just 2700 inhabitants on the island, this is a place to rest, recuperate, and really get away from it all, and you'll discover this as soon as you hit the unspoiled and picturesque beached on the island. We particularly love Keel Bay.

(http://achilltourism.com)

35. Wave a Rainbow Flag at Dublin Pride

Dublin has an LGBT community that is loud and proud. To celebrate all the achievements that the community has achieved up until now, and to push for further visibility, the city's LGBT people get together and wave their rainbow flags with pride all over Dublin. Gay Pride in Dublin is a whole week of events, but the highlight is always the Saturday parade, when floats parade along the streets of the city centre to pumping pop music. This is a fantastic event to be part of whether you are gay or not. *(http://dublinpride.ie)*

36. Catch a Ceilidh at Crane Bar in Galway

The Irish have a reputation as a nation of people who love to party and celebrate, and of course, it can be a wonderful idea to join in with the festivities on your visit. And that means you simply need to know about Crane Bar in Galway, one of the best known and loved traditional music pubs in the city. There is live traditional music on every night of the week, so even if you want to party and experience a ceilidh on a Sunday night, that's something you can do at Crane Bar.

(2 Sea Rd, Galway; www.thecranebar.com)

37. Eat a Picnic by the Ruins of Inch Abbey

These days, as you walk up to the 12th century Inch Abbey on the north bank of the Quoile River, you don't get to see an abbey as it would have been all those centuries ago, but we think the ruins of this dishevelled abbey are truly just as charming. Honestly, there's not a whole day's worth pf exploring to do, but if you find yourself in Ireland on a sunny day and are looking for a quaint picnic spot, we think sitting on the grass in front of the ruins is something very special indeed.

(Inch Abbey Rd, Downpatrick)

38. Watch a Spinning Demo at the Sheep & Wool Centre

As you meander around Ireland's countryside, you will soon notice that there are many sheep who live on this land, and this means that there's a huge wool and textile industry in the country. If you'd really like to get to grips with this, the Sheep & Wool Centre in Connemara is the place to be. At this museum, you can follow the process from shearing to yarn, and you can even see live demonstrations of sheep being sheared, and yarn being spun.

(Connemara Loop, Letterbrickaun, Connemara, Co. Galway; www.sheepandwoolcentre.com)

39. Discover Ancient Artefacts at the National Museum of Ireland

History buffs are going to be positively bowled away by the National Museum of Ireland, where the highlight has to be the selection of incredible artefacts that have been dug up from archaeological excavations. There are collections of prehistoric metals and gold, an exhibition that explores the myths from the Battle for Dublin, Bronze Age Irish tools and weaponry, and lots more besides. There are often talks about the various collections, and drop-in activities for kids as well. *(Kildare St, Dublin 2; www.museum.ie/Home)*

40. Ride the Waves of Bundoran

When you think of surfing capitals of the world, you might think of places in Hawaii or California, but if you fancy riding the waves off the coast of Ireland, there is no chance of you leaving disappointed. There are numerous awesome surf spots dotted around the country, and Bundoran, a small town in County Donegal, might just be the best of them. There are six surf schools in the town that cater to all abilities, so give it a go even if you're a total beginner.

41. Fill Your Stomach at McCambridge's Food Hall

When it's lunchtime in Galway and you want to seek out something delicious to put into your stomach, the number one place to be has to be McCambridge's Food Hall, which is distinctly Irish but has a bit of something to appeal to everyone. Once inside, you'll be bowled over by the choice of Irish meat, seafood, cheese, and charcuterie. Whiskies are also a specialty at McCambridge's, and when is there a better time for a midday tipple than when you're on

holiday?

(38-39 Shop St, Galway; https://mccambridges.com)

42. Hike The Kerry Way Trail

If you are really serious about walking, you need to know about The Kerry Way. But don't think that this is some kind of afternoon hike, it's actually a 200km signposted trail that starts at finishes in scenic Kilkenny. The lovely thing about this trail is that you have the opportunity to traverse all kinds of terrain, from tarmac roads through to trails in the mountains. The trail typically takes 9 days to complete, it's a feat of physical endurance, and it's 100% worth the effort.

(www.kerryway.com)

43. Feel Ireland's History at Donegal Castle

Donegal Castle, situated in the centre of Donegal town, was built by chieftains called the O'Donnells in the 15th century, watching out over the River Eske. In the 16th century, the castle was rebuilt in the Jacobean style by Basil Brooke after O'Donnell burned his own castle to the ground when it fell into enemy hands. Now you can catch daily tours that illustrate the history of the castle, and that give you the opportunity to take in its stunning interiors.

(Tyrconnell Street, Milltown, Donegal)

44. Enjoy a Fishing Trip on Lough Derg

The third largest lake in all of Ireland, Lough Derg is a freshwater lake with an area of 130km. It's a perfectly picturesque place to hang out and enjoy some low-key tranquillity, but it's also a wonderful place for a spot of lake fishing. The good news is that you don't need a license to fish on Lough Derg, and there are fishing boats to rent all around, so getting your catch of the day (there's lots of brown trout and pike in the lake) couldn't be easier. *(www.loughderg.org)*

45. Down a Pint in Ireland's Oldest Pub

The Brazen Head is a pub in Dublin that dates way back to 1198, and that makes it the oldest pub in all of Ireland, and a really special place for a leisurely pint. Beyond the feeling of history and tradition that you will have as soon as you take a stool at the bar, this is a great place for a fun evening. The owners have entertainment practically every night of the week, whether in the form of live storytelling, Irish fiddle music, or local folk bands.

(20 Lower Bridge St, Merchants Quay, Dublin 8; www.brazenhead.com)

46. Learn About Cork's History at Cork Public Museum

If you find yourself in Cork on a drizzly day, we can't think of a better way to pass a morning than at the Cork Public Museum. The artefacts inside the museum will take you on a journey from the Stone Age right up to the present day. Inside, some of the highlights include excavations from the medieval city walls, Bronze Age tools from copper mines, Iron Age helmet horns, and even an exhibition on Irish Traveller culture.

47. Find Something Special at Donegal Craft Village

Situated just outside of Donegal town, the Donegal Craft Village is the ultimate souvenir shopping destination in Ireland. Here you can meet local artisans who work in many different media, with textiles, glassware, ceramics, crystal, woodwork, and more besides. This is a chance to get to know the makers, appreciate Irish craft, learn the stories behind beautiful items, and take home some one of a kind items for your home.

(Lurganboy, Donegal; www.donegalcraftvillage.com)

48. Go Windsurfing on Culdaff Beach

For those with an adventurous spirit, Ireland is a country that offers up all kinds of adventures, and it doesn't get much more adventurous that windsurfing over Culdaff Beach. The beach itself is incredible but it's the waves that draw visitors to this stretch of the Irish coastline year after year. There are a few schools at this beach that can take you through the whole process and help you unleash your inner adventurous spirit.

49. Enjoy the Cape Clear Island Storytelling Festival

Ireland is a country with many stories from its past, and you can fully appreciate the many stories of this nation if you visit the Cape Clear Island Storytelling Festival, which takes place at the beginning of September each year. Of course, the festival contains many storytelling events for old and young, there are numerous concerts during the festival, and you can even enjoy a storytelling boat trip.

50. Watch a Concert at Ulster Hall

If you find yourself in Belfast and aren't sure what to do in the evening time, you can practically guarantee that you will be entertained if you visit Ulster Hall, a B1 listed building that first opened all the way back in 1862. This concert venue has played host to a remarkable number of gigs, and it was, in fact, the first place that Led Zeppelin ever played "Stairway to Heaven". These days, it's a place where you can catch a rock gig, a symphony orchestra, and even comedy performances.

(34 Bedford St, Belfast; www.ulsterhall.co.uk)

51. Be Wowed by the Glencar Waterfall

Glencar waterfall is where nature meets culture in Ireland. Although it is indeed a very beautiful waterfall (and particularly so after rainfall), Glencar waterfall, which can be found in County Leitrim, is also famous because it was a place that the iconic poet W.B Yeats visited often in his youth, and the waterfall is even mentioned in a poem of his called "The Stolen Child". There are picnic facilities right by the waterfall, and it's also a perfect spot for an al fresco lunch.

52. Have an Artsy Day at the Limerick City Gallery of Art

Ireland is often thought to be more of a historic place than a hub of contemporary culture, but if you are the artsy sort, we don't think the country will disappoint. The Limerick City Gallery of Art is one of the leading contemporary galleries in the whole country, and a superb place to spend a couple of hours. This is a place to really get to grips with artworks by Irish artists, and the collection contains works from the 18th, 19th, 20th, and 21st centuries.

(Carnegie Building, Pery Square, Limerick; http://gallery.limerick.ie)

53. Find Peace and Quiet in the National Botanic Gardens

As a small city of just around 1 million people, Dublin doesn't have the hustle and bustle of some other capital cities. Still, if you want to experience perfect quietude, it's a great idea to spend a peaceful morning in the National Botanic Gardens, which lie just 5km outside of the main city. Dating way back to the 19th century, the 19 acres of land here contains an incredible selection of biodiversity, with more than 20,000 living plants.

(Glasnevin, Dublin 9; www.botanicgardens.ie)

54. Get Boozed Up at the Irish Beer & Whiskey Festival

It's no secret that the Irish like a tipple, no matter the day of the week. As the saying goes, if you can't beat 'em, join 'em, and that's exactly what you are invited to do at the annual Irish Beer & Whiskey Festival, which takes place around St Paddy's Day every year in Dublin. The festival is raucous, and a true celebration of everything Irish, with copious amounts of whiskey, local beers, ciders, and live music.

(www.irishbeerandwhiskeyfestival.com)

55. Discover Irish Life From the Stone Age

If you're the kind of person who gets bored at the idea of trawling through aisle after aisle of musty museums, we think that the Irish National Heritage Park in Wexford might just be the kind of museum that you can actually get on board with. The difference with this place is that it's an open-air museum that really brings history to life. As you walk through the 35 hectares, you'll actually see Ireland as it was since the Stone Age, through the Norman period, and more.

(Newtown, Ferrycarrig, Co. Wexford; www.inhp.com)

56. Take a Boat Trip to the Saltee Islands

Located about 5 kilometres off the coast of County Wexford, the Saltee Islands make for the perfect day trip when you want to get away from it all. These islands are actually owned by one family, and visitors are only allowed 11.30am and 4.30pm, but fortunately there are many tour companies that can take you there. The islands are particularly renowned for their birdlife, and if you are lucky, you might even see puffins on your trip.

57. Chow Down on Fish & Chips in Cork

A trip to Ireland is not a trip to Ireland if you fail to tuck into a hearty place of fish and chips. Of course, you'll be able to find this deliciousness right around the country, but for our money, The Fish Wife in Cork might just serve up the best fish and chips supper in all of Ireland. If you really want an indulgent experience, the Fish Box with cod, hake, and smoked haddock is 100% the way to go. *(45 MacCurtain Street, Montenotte, Cork; www.thefishwifetakeaway.com)*

58. Buy Wild Honey and Candles From Brookfield Farm

Before you depart from the green pastures of Ireland, you'll surely want to grab some souvenirs to remind you of this beautiful country, but take our advice and avoid the cheesy souvenir shops and head to Brookfield Farm in County Tipperary instead. But this is a farm with a difference because it's a bee farm. At this farm, you'll get to try the most beautiful wild blossom honey and you can take away authentic beeswax candles.

(www.brookfieldfarm.org)

59. Sip on Irish Craft Beers at 57 The Headline

Everyone knows that Ireland is famous for its Guinness, and delicious as it is, there are times when you might want to try a different ale or beer. Cut to 57 The Headline, the premiere bar in Dublin for serving up local, Irish, craft beers. For somewhere that places an emphasis on locally produced beers, you might expect the bar to be overly trendy, but actually they have the best of both worlds - a beer menu that is thoroughly modern and an atmosphere that still feels like traditional Dublin.

(Clanbrassil Street Lower Clanbrassil Street Lower, Merchants Quay, Dublin 8; http://57theheadline.com)

60. Stay at a Private Retreat at Clew Bay

When you're on holiday, it's time to indulge and forget about the stresses and responsibilities of everyday life, and this is more than possible if you choose to stay on a luxury retreat on a private island. This is 100% possible if you choose to visit Clew Bay, which is said to have 365 islands, one for every day of the year. Collanmore Island is one of the largest, and a private island where you are invited to stay and enjoy the incredible decadence of the Collanmore Lodge.

(http://collanmorelodge.com)

61. Enjoy All the Fun of Puck Fair

With almost 400 years of documented evidence, Puck Fair is one of the oldest known festivals in Ireland. The fair starts on August 10th each year, and then lasts for three days. On the first day, a group of people goes into the mountains to catch a wild goat. It's then brought back to Kilorglin in County Kerry, a young schoolgirl names the goat "King Puck", it's put into a cage for three days, and its then led back to its mountain home, and everyone back in the town has an epic party. The reasoning behind the tradition isn't known, but it's still popular today.

(http://puckfair.ie)

62. Indulge at the Taste of West Cork Food Festival

If you are crazy about food and want to put as much deliciousness in your stomach as possible on your trip to Ireland, we highly recommend coinciding your trip away with the Taste of West Cork food festival, which is hosted in September each year. Tonnes of food producers are drawn to Cork at this time, and you can expect pop-up food markets, cooking demonstrations from leading Irish chefs, cookery competitions, and special dinners and banquets.

(www.atasteofwestcork.com)

63. Visit a Working Farm, Killary Sheep Farm

Rural life is something extremely important in Ireland, and to get to grips with this part of the local culture it can be a great idea to pay a visit to a working farm, and one of the friendliest that we have encountered has to be the Killary Sheep Farm. The staff at the farm arrange their own countryside walks so you can discover some of the local beauty, there are sheep shearing demonstrations in the summer months, and sheep dog demonstrations too.

64. Enjoy the Views From the Cliffs of Moher

The Cliffs of Moher are one of the most stunning natural features we have ever seen, and we feel confident that you'll be bowled away by them as well. Located in the Burren region of County Clare, these cliffs extend for 8 kilometres, and are 214 metres tall at their highest. A lookout point that was created in 1835 offers spectacular views over the surrounding areas, and on a clear day you can see as far as the Aran Islands in Galway Bay.

65. Have a Luxury Stay in a Historic Castle

During your time in Ireland, it's likely that you'll see your fair share of castles, and many of those castles will be very impressive, but how much cooler would it be if you could stay the night in a castle? Well, you can! Dromoland is a 19th century castle you can find in County Clare, but these days it's a 5 star hotel where you can expect luxury piled on to luxury. The castle has had many famous guests, including Jack Nicholson, Johnny Cash, and Nelson Mandela.

(Dromoland, Newmarket-on-Fergus, Co. Clare; www.dromoland.ie)

66. Get Close to the Animals at Fota Wildlife Park

On a day trip to Fota Wildlife Park, which lies about 20 minutes outside of Cork, you might be forgiven for thinking that you have found yourself in the tropics, because there are many exotic animals that can be found in this park. Bring your kids along and they will have the opportunity to get up close to emus, ostriches, zebras, cheetahs, black spider monkeys, and the Asiatic lion.

(Foaty, Carrigtwohill, Co. Cork; www.fotawildlife.ie)

67. Experience Your Best Ever St Patrick's Day

St Patrick's Day is a celebration of the patron Saint of Ireland, which falls on March 17th each year. You have no doubt celebrated St Patrick's Day in your own country and had a whale of a time, so can you imagine just how incredible the experience is in the Irish capital city? In Dublin, Paddy's Day involves more than just a swift pint of Guinness in the pub. There will be a parade that dominates the city streets, a funfair, music concerts in the street, and, of course, lots of parties that will have you dancing all night long.

68. Have a Sea Kayaking Adventure at Inchydoney

What better way to explore the coastline of Ireland than to actually get out there on the water? This is something that you can do at Inchydoney, a small island off the coast of west Cork, where sea kayaking is a very popular activity. The sea here is very calm, and this is an activity that can suit all ages and fitness abilities. We guarantee that after a morning of sea kayaking on the open water, you will feel like a different person.

69. Take a Tour of Cork City Gaol

Walking through the aisles of a former prison might seem like a grizzly thing to do on your vacation, but if you have an interest in Ireland's social history, we think that it's well worth the effort. Cork City Gaol opened in the 1820s and housed prisoners from within the city boundaries. The very good audio tour of the prison will give you a lesson in just how terrible life was for prisoners a century ago with hardly anything to eat and hours and hours of hard labour. *(Convent Ave, Sunday's Well, Cork; http://corkcitygaol.com)*

70. Relax at Ireland's Highest Waterfall

If you decide to take a day trip to Powerscourt House & Gardens, don't limit yourself to the grounds itself. Surrounding the house, there is a spectacular valley where you can get back to nature. The valley is home to something that nature lovers will love – Ireland's highest waterfall, which has a height of 121 metres. There is also a kiosk set close by to the waterfall, so if you want to make a day of it and grab a hot dog or an ice cream while you enjoy the waterfall, you are welcome to do so.

71. Sample Dublin Delicacies at Taste of Dublin

Dublin is increasingly being thought of as a foodie city, but eating out in restaurants for breakfast, lunch, and dinner can be expensive. If you want to taste the best that

Dublin has to offer but restaurant hopping isn't in your budget, you need to know about Taste of Dublin. This food festival takes place every June, and each year the best restaurants from around the city showcase their signature dishes, there is an artisan market, and you can watch cooking demonstrations from local chefs as well. *(http://dublin.tastefestivals.com)*

72. Keep the Kids Entertained at Blackrock Castle

Travelling with kids can be challenging to say the least. There are many beautiful sights around Ireland, but you have to try and keep your kids entertained at all times. Blackrock Castle in Cork can please both adults and kids, because while it's a beautiful historic castle, the interior has been transformed into an observatory and interactive science museum. Your kids can even go on an interactive space mission and make decisions to change its course. *(Castle Rd, Blackrock, Co. Cork; www.bco.ie)*

73. Stroll Through the Iconic Trinity College

Dublin is full of iconic buildings but there is none more famous than Trinity College. It is one of the seven ancient universities of Britain, and walking around the campus is like stepping back in time since the university dates back to the 16th century. The college grounds cover 47 acres of land, so it can be a great idea to go on a guided tour so that you can fully get to grips with the history and significance of this important part of Irish academia.

(College Green, Dublin 2; www.tcd.ie)

74. Hit a Few Golf Balls at the New Ross Golf Club

If your idea of a perfect getaway is packing up your clubs and hitting a few golf balls, Ireland certainly isn't going to disappoint as there are plenty of mightily impressive golf courses over this green land. The New Ross Golf Club is over 100 years old, and can be found in the picturesque Wexford area. Just try not to be put off your game by the stunning Brandon and Blackstairs mountains in the background.

(Tinnakilly Big, New Ross, Co. Wexford; www.newrossgolfclub.ie)

75. Sample Local Cheeses at Sheridan's Cheesemongers

Ireland is a country full of greenery, which means there is lots of farming and wonderful food produce. For this reason, it's imperative that you tuck into as much local grub as is humanly possible on your trip to Ireland's capital. If you are a cheese fan, waste no time and head straight to Sheridan's Cheesemongers in Dublin. The staff are friendly, know their stuff, and will always let you try before you buy, so a visit to Sheridan's is the perfect place to sample the impressive breadth of Irish cheese making. *(11 Anne St S, Dublin 2; http://sheridanscheesemongers.com)*

76. Catch a Live Show at the Dublin Fringe Festival

Dublin has an incredible arts scene, and you can experience the full force of its creativity each year at the Dublin Fringe Festival. Held across two weeks every year in September, the city hosts more than 200 performances across the city. Whether you want to see some edgy physical theatre, or you want to laugh out loud at the newest standup comedy talent, there is something for you at the Dublin Fringe.

(www.fringefest.com)

77. Enjoy a Traditional Irish Tea in Galway

It is no secret that the Irish enjoy a cup of tea, and on a trip to Ireland, you need to treat yourself to a traditional afternoon tea at least once. There are teahouses dotted around the country just for this purpose, but we are especially fond of Cupan Tae in Galway. You can go traditional with Earl Grey tea and fluffy scones, or you can try something a little different as this house actually serves up more than fifty varieties of tea.

(8 Quay Ln, Galway; www.cupantae.eu)

78. Relax in a Suspended Cocoon

When you are on holiday, it can be great to take a day out for some indulgent spa treatments. There are hotels all over Dublin where you can get pampered with things like facials, scrubs, and body massages, but the spa in The Marker Hotel offers something very different indeed. This spa has two cocoons that are suspended from its ceiling. They are cushioned to perfectly take your body weight, and they are a relaxing place to read a book or have a cup of tea.

(Grand Canal Square, Docklands, Dublin 2; www.themarkerh)oteldublin.com/spa.html)

79. Warm Your Bones With a Bowl of Guinness Stew

Irish food is all about comfort and warming your bones from the inside out. We can't think of anything more comforting than a piping hot bowl of Guinness Stew. This stew is typically slow cooked with big hulks of beef, root vegetables, and, of course, Guinness, which gives the dish richness and depth. There are endless places where you can try a bowlful in Ireland, but we recommend the Brazen Head (the oldest pub in the country!), The Quays, and Arthur's Pub for the best Guinness stew in Dublin.

80. Learn Something New at the Cork Butter Museum

When you spread Irish butter on your toast for the first time and then take a bite, you will be wondering how Irish butter has managed to escape you for all these years. Of course, the best way of becoming acquainted with the good stuff is by eating it, but you can also learn more about local butter at the Cork Butter Museum. Inside, you can find lots of artefacts and documents that tell the story of butter trade in Ireland over the course of its history and right up to the present day.

(The Tony O'Reilly Centre, O'Connell Square, Shandon, Cork; www.corkbutter.museum)

81. Dance, Dance, Dance at Longitude Festival

If you love nothing more than to dance in puddles of mud while listening to live music from some of the most awesome bands on the planet, you need to get tickets to Dublin's Longitude Festival as a priority. Every July, Marlay Park, one of the largest parks in the city, invites world music talent to its stages so that thousands of merrymakers can dance until dawn. Highlights from previous years have been Massive Attack, The Chemical Brothers, Phoenix, and Major Lazer.

(www.longitude.ie)

82. Get to Grips with the Ireland's Literary History

Dublin is world famous on the literary scene. Many Dubliners, such as James Joyce, Oscar Wilde, and WB Yeats, have created some of the best loved works of literature ever written. To learn more about the Irish literary tradition, head straight to the Dublin Writers' Museum. As you tour the 18th century mansion, you can explore the lives and works of the writers through manuscripts, personal letters, their personal objects, and their books. Guided tours are also available.

(18 Parnell Square, Dublin)

83. Ride a Horse at the Slieve Aughty Riding Centre

There are numerous ways to explore the beautiful countryside of Ireland, but none is quite as special as mounting a horse and viewing this green land on horseback. There are numerous places where you can take a horse ride in Ireland, but we are particularly fond of the Slieve Aughty Riding Centre, which is set across 17 acres of land in County Galway. Whether you want to book a scenic ride for the afternoon or stay for a while and have a horse riding holiday, the choice is yours.

(Kylebrack West, Loughrea,, Co. Galway;
www.slieveaughtycentre.com)

84. Get Entertained at the Kilkenny Arts Festival

There are quite a few arts festivals dotted around the country during the year, but our favourite of these might just be the Kilkenny Arts Festival, which is hosted in Kilkenny in the middle of August each year. Founded in 1974 by a group of classical music enthusiasts, the festival now incorporates many kinds of performances and shows from poetry readings to contemporary dance, and everything in between. Performances are as likely to occur on the streets as in venues, and there is a parade through the streets every year as well.

(www.kilkennyarts.ie)

85. Take the Angela's Ashes Walking Tour

Before you visit Ireland, a must read is Angela's Ashes, an autobiography of Frank McCourt's life, which tells the story of how young Frank and his family tried to escape the poverty of pre-war Limerick. These days, you can actually step inside the book on a trip to Limerick by going on the Angela's Ashes walking tour, a tour that will take you to the streets where Frank grew up, the school where he had his education, the pub where he and his family drank, and the People's Park.

86. Spend the Night in Blackhead Lighthouse

There are plenty of lighthouses dotted around the country, but there aren't many that actually offer their own beds. Blackhead Lighthouse on the Country Antrim coastline is the exception to the rule, and if you fancy accommodation experience outside of the regular hotels and guesthouses. From your self catering accommodation, you will get to experience 360 degree panoramic views and watch as the tide goes in and out.

(20 Blackhead Path, Whitehead, Carrickfergus)

87. Discover 9000 Years of History at Ulster Museum

On a trip to Belfast, the Ulster Museum is a must visit place. Located in the city's Botanic Gardens, this museum first opened its doors in the 19th century, and has since garnered an epic collection of artefacts that detail 9000 years of history. There are numerous bizarre collections inside, including a collection of mounted birds from Sicily, an Egyptian mummified body of a woman, and art from Francis Bacon amongst many other items.

(Botanic Gardens, Belfast; http://nmni.com/um)

88. Chow Down at the Galway Oyster Festival

Ireland is, of course, an island, which means that it's surrounded by water, which in turn means that it is a place where you can eat lots of delicious seafood. If you can't get enough of the delights of the sea, we can recommend a trip to the Galway Oyster Festival, which is hosted annually on the last weekend on September. The festival contains a masquerade gala, oyster opening competitions, and even a silent disco, but the highlight is always sampling the local oysters, which are the best we've ever tasted.

(http://galwayoysterfestival.com)

89. Pick Fruit at Lamberts Fruit Farm

The summer is undoubtedly the best time of year to visit the Irish capital. Local people drink cans of cider in the park, cycle along the streets, and are generally more amiable. In the summertime, you can also take more trips out into the country. One short trip you can make is to Lambert's Fruit Farm, which lies just outside of Dublin. This is one of few farms that allows visitors to take a basket and pick as much fruit as they want during a set time. If you have a sweet tooth and want some country air, this is for you.

(Cruagh Lane, Rathfarnham Dublin 16)

90. Hike the Carrauntoohil Mountain

If you are serious about having some outdoor adventures during your time in Ireland, you need to know about the Carrauntoohil Mountain, which is the highest peak in

Ireland at 1038 metres high. Although it's the highest peak and climbing to the top does require a certain fitness level, you can get to the peak and back down again in 6 to 7 hours, so it's definitely doable for an adventurer. We recommend using a guide who is familiar with the trail, particularly if you're an inexperienced climber.

91. Expand Your Palette With a Horse Meat Sandwich

Have you ever felt so hungry that you could have eaten a horse? Well, would you be prepared to take the phrase literally? That's right, over at Paddy Jack in Temple Bar they serve up horsemeat sandwiches. It is a controversial choice, that is without a doubt, but the horse steak baguettes fly out the door, so there has to be something nice about them right? If you're a food adventurer, you should most definitely add this to your Dublin bucket list!

92. Go Fishing on the Easkey River

If your idea of the perfect trip away is sitting on the edge of a river for days on end with your fishing rod in the water, Ireland is the ultimate travel destination for you, and you need to become acquainted with the Easkey River. There are copious numbers of salmon and sea trout in these clean waters, and the best time for fishing is in the spring and summer months. You might just catch yourself dinner.

93. Get Artsy at the National Gallery of Ireland

If you have an interest in the visual arts, the National Gallery of Ireland should be right at the top of your "must visit" list on a trip to Dublin. The impressive museum holds over 15,000 items, and you'll be able to find paintings, sculptures, drawings, prints, photographs, and more inside. There are works from all over Europe, including art work from Monet, Caravaggio, and Rembrandt. This is also a budget conscious way to spend an afternoon as the audio guides that will take you around the museum's permanent collection are totally free.

(Merrion Square W, Dublin 2; www.nationalgallery.ie)

94. Walk Out to Inishkeel Island

Just off the coast of County Donegal, you can find an island called Inishkeel island, and at low tide a tidal bank is created so that you can actually walk across to the island. This isn't just a quaint thing to do, the island is actually fascinating, and houses the ruins of a 6th century ancient Christian settlement. You can also discover the ruins on two churches and a graveyard. Just be sure to make it off the island while the tidal bank still exists!

95. Feel Dublin's Creativity at the Irish Design Shop

Dublin is definitely one of the most traditional capital cities in the world, and most people don't visit the city for its cutting edge design, but this is not to say that Dublin doesn't have a creative scene. It most certainly does, and you can feel the force of that incredible creative spirit at the Irish Design Shop. It is the ideal place to go souvenir shopping for something that's a little out of the ordinary, and you'll find original works in ceramics, textiles, glassware, jewellery, and furniture from up and coming designers around the country.

(41 Drury St, Dublin 2; http://irishdesignshop.com)

96. Take in a Show at Cork Opera House

If you find yourself in the beautiful city of Cork and at a loss as to what to do in the evening time, a trip to the Cork Opera House could be just what you are looking for. This is probably the main performance space in Cork, and it has a long history that dates back to 1855 when its doors first opened. These days, you can find all kinds of performances on the stage of the Opera House so whether you would like to see a grand opera, a contemporary musical, or an elegant ballet, there will be something in the programme for you.

(Emmett Pl, Centre, Cork; www.corkoperahouse.ie)

97. Drink in Belfast's Most Famous Bar, Crown Liquor Saloon

Belfast certainly has no shortage of places to have a drink, but the Crown Liquor Saloon is without a doubt the most famous and most special of all the city's drinking haunts. Opened all the way back in 1885, the Crown Liquor Saloon is a stunning example of a Victorian gin palace. As you step inside, you are bound to be taken aback by the incredible interiors, which include a floor made with mosaic tiles, intricately brocaded walls, wooden columns, and ornate mirrors throughout.

(46 Great Victoria St, Belfast)

98. Be Bowled Over by King John's Castle in Limerick

In the city of Limerick, there is one stand out attraction: King John's Castle. This 13th century castle is picturesquely set against the waters of the Shannon River. This is actually one of the best preserved castles from this period of time in Europe, and when you visit you'll be able to see the towers, walls and fortifications more or less as they were back then. Kids won't be bored on a trip to the castle either, as there are interactive exhibitions and animations telling the castle's history inside.

(Nicholas St, Limerick;

www.shannonheritage.com/KingJohnsCastle)

99. Learn About Smoked Salmon at the Connemara Smokehouse

No trip to Ireland would be complete without chowing down on the delicious smoked salmon that comes from the country. A small village called Ballyconneely is the unlikely setting for smoked salmon aficionados in the country as it's where the Connemara Smokehouse is situated. No time is a bad time to visit this place and pick up some smoked salmon, but do check out their programme of events because you could also have demos in the smoking process.

(The Pier, Ballyconneely, Co. Galway; www.smokehouse.ie)

100. Take a Selfie With Oscar Wilde

Oscar Wilde is one of the most famous names to have ever emerged from the city of Dublin. Although Oscar Wilde passed away many years ago, you can see a statue of him in the corner of Merrion Square Park, one of Dublin's five Georgian squares. The memorial sees the figure of Wilde leaning back in a relaxed way, and it perfectly captures his playful character and essence. If you are a big

Oscar Wilde fan, why not take a selfie with the man himself?

101. Test Your Sea Legs at the Docklands Maritime Festival

If you love nothing more than to take in the fresh sea air, make sure that you attend the annual Docklands Maritime Festival in Dublin, which takes place every June Bank Holiday weekend. You can expect majestic ships that you can tour, street performances on the docks, and an incredible outdoor market where you can purchase anything from local crafts to delicious street eats. The festival attracts more than 100,000 visitors each year, so make sure you are one of them.

(www.docklandssummerfestival.com)

Before You Go...

Thanks for reading **101 Amazing Things to Do in Ireland.** We hope that it makes your trip a memorable one!

Have a great trip, and don't drink too much Guinness!
Team 101 Amazing Things

Made in the USA
Monee, IL
12 December 2024